His Name is John Son of Elizabeth and Zacharias

ISBN: 978-1-964452-01-2 (hc)
ISBN: 978-1-964452-00-5 (sc)
ISBN: 978-1-964452-02-9 (e)

Library of Congress Control Number: 2024909381

Printed in the United States of America

05/03/2024

His Name is John Son of Elizabeth and Zacharias

Adam E. Oblad

Elizabeth and Zacharias had been married for many years. They believed in God and listened for the righteous promptings they received from Him.

Zacharias and Elizabeth said their prayers each day and tried to always follow the rules.

Zacharias and Elizabeth were getting old, and sadly, they had been unable to have children of their own. They spent their time cheerfully serving others while longing to be parents.

One day a miracle happened while Zacharias was working as a priest in the temple.

Zacharias was praying and burning incense to worship God.

Clouds of smoke from the incense were floating in the air and slowly rising toward the ceiling.

What do you think the rising smoke is symbolic of?

As the incense burned, the smoke rose toward heaven. Zacharias was hopeful that his prayers would rise upward to heaven like the smoke from the incense. Suddenly, while Zacharias was praying, he noticed an angel standing near the altar, where the incense was burning.

Zacharias was afraid, and the angel said to him, "Fear not." The angel also explained that God had heard the prayers that had been offered by Elizabeth and Zacharias. The angel told Zacharias that his wife, Elizabeth, would bear a son and that his name would be John and that Elizabeth and Zacharias shall have joy and gladness with their child.

The angel said that many shall rejoice at his birth, for he shall be a great teacher and shall be filled with the Holy Ghost. The angel told Zacharias that John would be sent from heaven to help the people as they prepared for the arrival of the Messiah.

Zacharias knew that his wife was too old to have a baby, and he was having trouble believing what the angel had shared with him. Zacharias asked the angel to show him a sign, to help him believe that what the angel had prophesied would really come to pass.

The angel said that his name was Gabriel and that he was sent from the presence of God to give this joyful message to Zacharias. The angel explained to Zacharias that a sign would be given to him, because he failed to believe in what the angel had said. Zacharias would be unable to speak until after the baby was born.

After the angel left, Zacharias noticed that he was unable to speak.

He left the temple and returned home to share this wonderful news with his wife, Elizabeth.

They rejoiced together that they would finally have a child born into their family. Zacharias was unable to speak, and so he would write down letters for others to read.

Eventually the time arrived, and the baby boy was born. A few days later, it was time to give the baby a name. The friends and relatives of Zacharias and Elizabeth gathered around for the baby to be named.

Everyone thought the baby should be named after his father, Zacharias.

Another miracle happened when Elizabeth was trying to explain that her baby would not receive the name of Zacharias, like his father's name.

And it came to pass that Zacharias was finally able to speak, and can you guess what he said?

Zacharias said, "His name is John!"

John grew up and became a spiritual leader. He was able to have God's spirit with him all the time, and he taught the people about someone special who was coming, someone who would baptize the people with fire and with the Holy Ghost.

What does it mean to be baptized? In the third chapter of Luke, Jesus shows us the way and teaches us about the importance of baptism. Jesus often taught people by showing them what to do and how to live.

John taught that a special person was coming soon and to prepare. This special person would be known as the Messiah, which means "Savior of the world." John was helping the people to get ready for the Messiah and the wonderful truths He would teach them.

John taught the people about repentance. John said that we all make mistakes.

What does that mean? How do we make mistakes? A mistake is doing something that we feel bad about, like being mean or breaking the rules.

John taught that we all become dirty from the mistakes that we make.

John began teaching by the river and was known among the people as a prophet.

The people wondered how they could become clean, and John taught them how. John told the people to apologize for their mistakes.

John said we all need to repent or apologize for our mistakes. We need to say "I'm sorry" if we hurt someone or break the rules.

John taught that we need to be washed clean with water.

20

John washed the people in the river, which is known as being baptized.

One day, John was teaching the people and washing them in the river.

Jesus was also there among the people.

John explained to the people that Jesus was the Messiah. Jesus was the special one that John had been teaching them about.

Jesus had not made any mistakes, but he wanted to be baptized. Jesus had been praying, and His Father in heaven asked Jesus to visit John and get baptized in the river.

Jesus asked John to baptize Him.

John knew that Jesus was special. John knew that Jesus was the Messiah, the Savior of the world.

John baptized Jesus, which means John took Jesus into the river and washed Jesus in the water.

Jesus showed us how important baptism is by getting baptized, so we all could follow His example.

Can you guess how old Jesus was when he was baptized?

He was about thirty years old.

Once Jesus was baptized, he began teaching the people to believe in Him and to believe in His Father in heaven, Who sent Jesus to live on our earth. Jesus taught the people many lessons about how to be kind to one another.

Jesus was always kind and patient with everyone. Jesus taught the people how they should live by providing everyone with a living example—a perfect model of love and humanity for each of us to follow.

The scriptures explain that a Messiah would come to save the people, and that day had finally arrived. Jesus, our Messiah, was finally there, among the people. Jesus would soon begin teaching the people how to live, how to pray, and how to be holy.

John taught the people the importance of repentance and baptism. John came to prepare the people for Jesus, our Messiah.

How special John must have been to be the one chosen to baptize the Messiah, the Savior of the world. In the Gospel of Matthew, verse 11 of chapter 11, Jesus honored John and John's mission of making ready the people for the coming Messiah, even Jesus Christ.

Jesus said these kind words about John: "Verily I say unto you, Among them that are born of women, there has not risen a greater than John the Baptist."

What will Jesus say about you?

About the Author

Adam Oblad is an identical twin and native of Utah (located in North America). Some of his favorite things include hiking, stargazing, aviation, and exploring the beautiful outdoors. Adam believes drawing near to Jesus is an important part of this life. He enjoys being a husband and father, and sharing heavenly truths with young readers and their parents.